IN THE
BEGINNING

IN THE
BEGINNING

Short conversations in Genesis

PAUL TAYLOR

AMBASSADOR INTERNATIONAL
Greenville, South Carolina • Belfast, Northern Ireland

IN THE BEGINNING
Short Conversations in Genesis

© Copyright 2008 Paul Taylor

NB. Unless otherwise stated, Bible text and quotations are from the NKJV

ISBN 978-1-84030-199-1

Ambassador Publications
a division of
Ambassador Productions Ltd.
Providence House
Ardenlee Street,
Belfast,
BT6 8QJ
Northern Ireland
www.ambassador-productions.com

Emerald House
427 Wade Hampton Blvd.
Greenville
SC 29609, USA
www.emeraldhouse.com

List of Contents

1

Fig Leaves and Animal Skins

Everybody knows that Adam and Eve wore fig leaves. But, as usual, what everybody knows is not quite correct. Adam and Eve only wore fig leaves for a very short time, after they had sinned.

Why wear leaves?

Once they had sinned, Adam and Eve knew that they were naked. This had not been a problem to them before they had sinned, but now they felt the need to cover their nakedness, which was symbolic of their guilt. Adam and Eve were now separated from God. As God walked in the Garden in the cool of the day, Adam and Eve hid. Today, we do not have full fellowship with God, because we also have sinned, and are guilty.

We try to cover our own guilt

Adam and Eve did this by sewing fig leaves together. These garments, they hoped, would cover their nakedness. In a similar way, we try to cover our own guilt by our own actions.

However, God covered Adam and Eve's guilt differently; He gave them garments of skin. (Genesis 3:21). God deliberately killed animals to make more suitable clothes to cover Adam and Eve's nakedness. This was the first time that animals had been killed. This shedding of blood was a forerunner of when Jesus was to shed His blood for us, once for all, on the cross.

God promised Jesus

As God cursed the serpent, He promised "I will put enmity between you and the woman, and between your seed and her Seed; He shall bruise your head, And you shall bruise His heel." The Seed of the Woman was to save us – by crushing the serpent's head. Jesus is that promised Seed of the Woman. How can we be sure? Children are described in the Bible as the seed of the father. Yet God was promising one day that there would be a Seed of the Woman – that is a clear prediction of the Virgin Birth. One day, says God, there will be a descendent of Adam and Eve, who does not have an earthly father, but who does have an earthly mother. Only Jesus fits that description.

2

Good News, Bad News

Jesus has come to bring us life. That is because without Jesus we just have death. In 1 Corinthians 15:55, 56 we read: "O death, where is your sting? O Hades where is your victory? The sting of death is sin."

When a wasp stings you, it is the poison in the sting that causes the pain. Those allergic to it will die. Some animals' stings can bring death. The poison that causes Death (with a capital D!) to the entire human race is Sin. "The sting of death is sin".

Jesus came to provide the antidote for that poison. But how can we accept an antidote, if we don't know that we have a problem in the first place. The Good News of Jesus makes no sense without first knowing the Bad News that makes Jesus' work necessary.

Romans 5:12 says "Through one man sin entered the world, and death through sin, and this death spread to all men, because all sinned". Some

Christians say that they believe Genesis, but they don't believe it is literal. They don't believe Adam was necessarily a real person. He was a myth, or a legend, or a symbol—symbolising the original sin of all mankind.

Does 1 Corinthians 15:22 say:

"For as in **a symbol** all die, even so **in Christ** all shall be made alive."?

How can we compare what Jesus **really** did for us on the cross, with what a **symbol** did in a mythological Genesis?

"For as in *a myth* all die, even so in Christ all shall be made alive."

1 Corinthians describes Jesus as the "last Adam." For the comparison to work, there must have been a first Adam.

God created Adam to enjoy fellowship with Him. He walked with him in the garden, in the cool of the day. When Adam sinned, that fellowship was broken.

When Jesus died, the curtain in the temple was torn in two from top to bottom. We can now go into the presence of God, and enjoy fellowship with Him once again, because Jesus has undone the

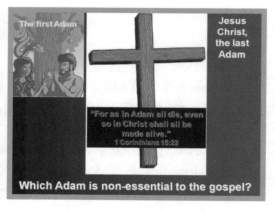

Which Adam is non-essential to the gospel?

power of sin and death. If we repent and turn to Him, He is ready and willing to save us. But if Adam's sin was not real, but only mythological or symbolic, then surely Jesus' salvation is likewise only symbolic. The Bad News is that there was actually a real Adam, who sinned and broke our fellowship with God. The Good News is that Jesus is the Last Adam, restoring our fellowship with God, if we will just turn to Him.

3

God's Rainbow

Rainbows are beautiful. Even our scientific understanding of them does not detract from their beauty.

Isaac Newton showed, in his famous experiment, that white light is a mixture of colours, which can be separated. Because different coloured lights have different wavelengths, they can be refracted, or bent, when travelling into or out of a glass prism ("Toblerone" shape).

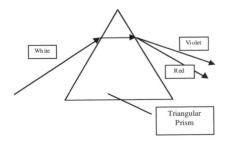

Red light is bent, or refracted, more than blue or violet light. Although we talk about the so-called "seven colours of the rainbow" (red, orange, yellow, green, blue, indigo, violet), in fact the spectrum or rainbow produced is a continuum of colours – it is not possible to work out where red ends and orange begins.

Rainbows are spectra produced by the light being refracted by spherical drops of water instead of triangular prisms. If we face a rainbow, then the sun is always behind us. This is because the light is being bent back towards us, by a combination of refraction and reflection.

Although the physics behind how a rainbow is produced is well understood, it is easy for us to overlook something in the description of the rainbow in Genesis 9:13 "I have set My rainbow in the cloud". The rainbow belongs to God. And the reason He has placed it there is given in the second part of the verse: "it shall be for the sign of the covenant between Me and the earth."

God has set up a covenant – an agreement – with everyone on the earth, whether we realise it or not. Every time we see a rainbow, it should remind us, and remind God, that "the waters shall never again become a flood to destroy all flesh." (Genesis 9:15) This is good news for us, and indicates the care that God has for this world.

We have seen before in these columns that the Flood was God's judgment on the pre-Flood world. It was the judgment of God for sin. The rainbow is symbolic of God's good news that He was able to rescue some people – Noah and his family – from the Flood.

2 Peter 3:10-13 reminds us that there is a judgment to come – a judgment this time, not by water, but by fire. Yet God still gives us the good news that we can be rescued through that judgment. His sign for this New Covenant is not the rainbow – it is the Cross. Jesus, the sinless Son of God, shed His own blood on the Cross, to pay the price for our sins, and to reconcile us to God.

4

A Whale of a Tale

The recent 'visit' of a bottle-nosed whale up the River Thames to the centre of London, and the intense international media interest, prompts a number of questions, such as 'Why has there been such an outpouring of popular emotion over this creature of the sea?' This is not to suggest that there was anything wrong in wishing the animal well. Nothing would have pleased me more than if the new story had ended with the whale swimming off into the North Sea. Yet there is a disturbing anthropomorphism that creeps into such news stories, born of our current society's evolutionary mindset.

What do whales and swans have in common? There are two answers to this question. In the UK, all whales and swans are owned by the Queen! The Crown claimed ownership of all swans in the 12th Century, but whales within three miles of the UK shore were not taken under Royal Patronage until a statute of 1324, under which whales are classed as 'fishes royal'. King Edward II declared 'Also the King shall have ... whales and sturgeons taken in the sea or elsewhere within the realm'. Today, whales are classed as mammals, rather than fish, yet the other thing that whales, sturgeon and swans have in common is that they were all created on the fifth day of creation, whereas land animals and people were created on the sixth day. This gives us our correct perspective on whales, and enables us to draw these two conclusions.

The first conclusion is that the cultural mandate of Genesis 1:28 ('Be fruitful and multiply; fill the earth and subdue it; have dominion over the fish of the sea, over the birds of the air, and over every living thing that moves on the earth') suggests that we should take care of whales, and not cause them to suffer, but not be sentimental either—certainly not considering that they are in some way an equivalent species to humanity.

Secondly, we are reminded once more that evolutionary theory cannot be 'fitted in' to the true creation account in Genesis. Evolutionists suppose that whales evolved from land-based mammals, so that the land mammals preceded aquatic mammals. The Bible makes clear that whales were created the day before land animals, so the evolutionary order is wrong in comparison with the Genesis account.

5

Power, Wisdom and Discretion in Creation

We are accustomed to seeing the worship of modern idols around us. Modern idols are not necessarily made of wood or stone. Today's objects of worship that people put in place of God are of various types. Some of these idols have four wheels. Some idols only really exist on CD or MTV. Other idols are less physically substantial—they may comprise of large bank balances, or the desire for large bank balances.

Modern Idols

Some modern idols would be more recognisable to people of biblical times. These objects of worship might be charms, horoscopes or crystals.

Sometimes, like the Children of Israel, Christians too can be tempted by such idols. In every case, idolatry leads an individual away from the worship of God.

While you might agree with all that I have written so far, you might wonder what all this has to do with Answers in Genesis. Is it part of our ministry to warn against idolatry?

In Jeremiah chapter 10 we read this:

> Thus you shall say to them: "The gods that have not made the heavens and the earth shall perish from the earth and from under these heavens."
> He has made the earth by His power, He has established the world by His wisdom, and has stretched out the heavens at His discretion. (Jeremiah 10:11,12)

Our attitude to such idols should be to note that they did not make the universe. Although this point should be obvious to us, the contrast with the True God could not be greater. God was not just standing back and watching the world evolve. Instead, as Jeremiah said, "He has made the earth by His power, He has established the world by His wisdom, and has stretched out the heavens at His discretion." (Emphasis mine).

Only God has the power to create

Only God has the power to create, and the Bible reminds us that he created the whole universe in just six days about 6,000 years ago. The way He created demonstrates His wisdom. The dynamics of the way the universe was made show His Sovereign choice. Compared to God, the false gods and idols look so worthless. What is the test of whether they are false or not? The test is to ask whether they created the heavens and the earth. Modern idols, like their older counterparts, did not make the heavens and the earth. Our God is the God who did make the heavens and the earth. He is worthy of all our worship as the only true God.

6

Before the Flood

The Bible is very clear why the Flood came.

> Then the LORD saw that the wickedness of man was great in the
> earth, and that every intent of the thoughts of his heart was only
> evil continually. And the LORD was sorry that He had made man
> on the earth, and He was grieved in His heart. So the LORD said,
> "I will destroy man whom I have created from the face of the
> earth, both man and beast, creeping thing and birds of the air, for
> I am sorry that I have made them." (Genesis 6:5-7)

The Flood was sent as a worldwide punishment for people's sins. The
fact that people had sinned greatly is seen in the accounts of various lives at

the end of Genesis. For example, Cain's great great great grandson, Lamech, took two wives for himself. Thus we have the beginning of polygamy, which so plagued various characters of the Old Testament—even God's servants, such as David and Solomon. Lamech also boasted about his power.

> "For I have killed a man for wounding me, even a young man for hurting me. If Cain shall be avenged sevenfold, then Lamech seventy-sevenfold." (Genesis 4:23-24)

The difference was that it was God who promised vengeance on those who were to harm Cain. Lamech, five generations on, was promising his own retribution. He was putting himself in the place of God. He was claiming for himself the right to exact an unbalanced revenge, where his retaliation would far outweigh the supposed wrong he had suffered. The Bible is not clear whether this was an idle boast, or a real threat. I suspect the latter, however, since Lamech had remarked that he had killed a man younger, therefore perhaps supposedly fitter, than himself.

There are many different ideas about who the sons of God and daughters of men mentioned in Genesis 6 were. This is perhaps not the place to address the controversy[1], except to note that there was careless, or carefree, marriage going on. Jesus reminded us that the days preceding His Second Coming would be similar.

> "For as in the days before the flood, they were eating and drinking, marrying and giving in marriage, until the day that Noah entered the ark, and did not know until the flood came and took them all away, so also will the coming of the Son of Man be." (Matthew 24:38-39)

---

1 My thoughts on the matter are contained in my book, *The Six days of Genesis*, published by Master Books.

Although the pre-Flood people did not know the exact day of the disaster that was to come, they were aware, or should have been aware, that it was coming, just as surely as Jesus will come again. God had already given them a 120-year warning:

> "My Spirit shall not strive with man forever, for he is indeed flesh; yet his days shall be one hundred and twenty years." (Genesis 6:3)

God has already warned our present generation that He will not always strive with mankind. There will be a reckoning—a Day of Judgment. The rest of Matthew 24 makes this clear. So why did God choose to save someone like Noah? Was it because he was a very good man?

No. It was because "Noah found grace in the eyes of the LORD" (Genesis 6:8). That is why the apostle Paul reminds us:

> For by grace you have been saved through faith, and that not of yourselves; it is the gift of God, not of works, lest anyone should boast. (Ephesians 2:8,9)

7

Preparing the Ark

Last month's article was about the state of the world before the Flood. I thought it would be useful this month to examine the preparations made before the Flood—about what God did and what Noah did.

Our English translations highlight an apparent contradiction in Genesis 6. We observed (chapter 6 'Before the Flood') that Noah was saved by grace, not by his righteousness (v8). This seems to be in contradiction to Noah being described as "perfect" in verse 9, until we realise that the Hebrew word translated as *perfect* actually means *blameless*.

God gave Noah a number of tasks to do, but other tasks were done by God Himself. For example, it was Noah's job to build the Ark. This clearly took a long time—it probably took most of the 120 years that God was allowing before the Flood was to come (Genesis 6:3). God gave Noah clear instructions on how to build the Ark. The instructions make sense. For example, one of the 'alternative' Flood legends—that of the Epic of Gilgamesh—has the Ark made like a cube. In the Bible, however, we have specific dimensions, in the proportions 300:50:30. This proportion is an excellent compromise between the considerations of comfort and stability for the vessel, and is approximately the same as many ships today. Noah's faithfulness, in building the Ark for more than a century before the Flood came, is celebrated in that well-known passage about faith, Hebrews 11 (v7). Hebrews 11 makes clear that Noah's righteousness was obtained by faith, not by good works.

The Ark was to be covered with 'pitch'. Precisely what the material was, we do not know—the Hebrew word simply means *covering*. The Ark was to be covered with a covering. However, the word is used elsewhere in Old Testament for the 'atonement'; the covering for sins provided by the blood sacrifice. This is why New Testament writers are able to see the Ark as a type of Christ. Just as the 'pitch' water-proofed the Ark against God's watery judgment, so the blood of Jesus 'fire-proofs' us from God's judgment to come.

After God's detailed instructions to Noah, He makes it clear that He is the One who is sending the Flood waters (Genesis 6:17). God then says "I will establish My covenant with you." This reminds us of Moses sprinkling the people with blood, announcing the "blood of the covenant". The Ark's atoning covering reminds us that salvation comes by God alone.

Another job given to Noah was to gather together all the food required for his family and all the animals. Fetching the animals themselves, however, was God's task. This reminds us that we have to make our own decisions, but that the actual works of grace are carried out by God alone. Another job that God reserved for Himself was shutting the door of the Ark. The salvation of Noah and his family was ultimately achieved without help from human beings, such as Noah. When we think about God's closing the door of the Ark to keep everyone safe within, we are reminded that Jesus said "I am the door.

If anyone enters by Me, he will be saved, and will go in and out and find pasture." (John 10:9) The Ark is a valuable reminder that there has only ever been one way of salvation, and that is through the blood of Jesus Christ.

8

Filling the Ark

It is often said that obviously Noah's Ark could not have been real. It would not be possible to fit so many animals on the Ark. After all, there are approximately 10 million species of animals on earth, so Noah would have needed space for 20 million animals. And wouldn't the woodworm have eaten the Ark?

Nowhere in the Bible does it actually say that Noah took two of every species. The word species is a comparatively modern term, owing much to the work of Carolus Linnaeus, the father of modern taxonomy. Linnaeus believed in the fixity of species, whereas today we see new species developing by means of natural selection rearranging or reducing the gene pool.

In fact, the Bible says that Noah was to receive two of every *kind* or *sort*. This concept of biblical *kind* is given the name *baramin* by creationist biologists, after the two Hebrew words meaning 'created kind'. These baramins are a much broader method of categorisation than mere species.

Furthermore, Noah was not to take two of every kind—he was only to take two of every mammal, two of every 'creeping thing'—referring to reptiles and two of every bird. All the animals taken on the Ark were vertebrates. They contained the *nephesh* life considered so important in Genesis 1, when God blessed certain kinds of animals. But not even every nephesh animal (i.e. those containing blood) were taken. There would be no need, for example, to take marine animals. This shows that the Flood must have been global, or there would also have been no point in Noah taking birds, because, if the Flood were local, they would have been able to fly away to dry land. Nor was there any need to take non-nephesh animals, such as invertebrates, including insects. In modern day flooding, it is often observed that insects and other invertebrates can survive on rafts of vegetation. It is very likely that invertebrates survived the Flood by similar methods.

One also needs to consider that the animals were of varying sizes. Dinosaurs need not have been as large as thought. Being reptilian in nature, it is possible that dinosaurs carried on growing as long as they lived. Therefore, large dinosaurs could have been old ones. Noah would therefore have taken smaller, younger dinosaurs on the Ark. Many dinosaurs and other animals were very small. The average size of the animals was probably the size of a sheep. These could easily have been kept apart in cages or enclosures, with plenty of space for food, and for removal of waste. It has been estimated that there would probably have been about 16,000 kinds, requiring 32,000 places in all. When one considers the enormous size of the Ark, we realise that 32000 sheep could easily be accommodated. Indeed, far from being over-crowded, it is likely that the Ark had room to spare.

It is noteworthy that Noah had to take seven (some versions suggest seven pairs) of *clean* animals. The fact that God could instruct Noah to take clean animals suggests that Noah would already know what was meant by this term, even though the biblical definition does not appear in print until the time of Moses. The purpose of this increased number of clean animals was so that Noah could offer a thank offering to God after the Flood. The fact that the provision for this thank offering was organised before the Flood shows Noah's faith that the Flood definitely would end, and that God would keep His promises. God always keeps His promises, so we can be sure that, if we have repented and put our trust in Jesus as our Lord and Saviour, that we will indeed be kept safe through the judgment to come and will be granted eternal life through Him.

9

The Floodwaters Rise

Imagine that the tide went out much further than it had ever done before. Imagine that you lived on a world full of evil, but this day, it seemed like something big was about to happen. One man and his family had been building an enormous vessel, while warning people of the coming judgment of God. You had joined in the laughter with everyone else. But now, there was a rumbling like thunder, the sky had strangely darkened, and water was falling like it had never fallen before. The largest tsunami the world has ever seen was heading your way.

Fanciful science fiction? According to the Bible, it is an event from the history of the world. In the last three articles, we have seen why the Ark was necessary, and how Noah went about preparing for the Flood. Now we need to examine how the Flood actually started.

In the six hundredth year of Noah's life, in the second month, the seventeenth day of the month, the same day were all the fountains of the great deep broken up, and the windows of heaven were opened. And the rain was upon the earth forty days and forty nights. (Genesis 7:11, 12)

The accuracy of the dating suggests a real event. Many commentators suggest that there may not have been rain before the Flood—Genesis 2:5 says "The LORD God had not caused it to rain on the earth". Rain drops require dust particles around which to coalesce. A good source of dust would be volcanic activity. This would seem to be suggested by the phrase "the fountains of the great deep were broken up". Vast resources of water beneath the crust would be thrown into the air, through these *fountains*—probably enormous volcanic activity—along with volcanic magma and dust. These fountains were as much a source of the Flood's water as the rain—the "windows of heaven" describing a deluge of water.

The waters rose, while the rain continued for 40 days. After the rain stopped, the waters continued to rise, due to geological upheaval for a further 50 days. Then the waters "prevailed" for a further 60 days, making a total of one hundred and fifty days (Genesis 7:24). The waters would then take a further 110 days to abate, and another 110 days to recede from the land. All these figures can be calculated from Genesis 7 and 8.

Why is it important to believe that this Flood happened? It is because it is important to believe God's word. Peter reminds us that, today, there are people who are "willingly ignorant" of the Flood (2 Peter 3:5). The fact of this great movement of God teaches us two things about God.

God is just

Galatians 6:7 reminds us that God is not mocked. "Whatever a man sows, that he will also reap." While it might seem for a season that evil men triumph, this does not go on forever. We are reminded that Noah was saved because he "found grace in the eyes of the LORD" (Genesis 6:8).

Equally important is the fact that:

God is merciful

The people had every opportunity to repent. God warned them of the Flood 120 years before it happened (Genesis 6:3). Even as the Flood was about to begin, God waited another seven days, before sending the rain (Genesis 7:4). He is truly the God who is "gracious, and full of compassion; slow to anger, and of great mercy" (Psalm 145:8)

10

How did Dinosaurs die?

A recent report in the Daily Telegraph (January 7th 2008) suggests that dinosaurs may have died out, because they were bitten to death by insects! For over twenty years, it has been more or less an article of faith that dinosaurs died out as a result of a massive asteroid strike on the Earth, supposedly near present day Mexico. Such an event is portrayed virtually as scientific fact, particularly in the popular media: - for instance, in the movie "The Land Before Time", or in the BBC's "documentary" series, "Walking With Dinosaurs". This catastrophic event, it is said, would have sent clouds of dust into the atmosphere, thus changing the climate and making it unwelcoming to dinosaurs. What is immediately noteworthy about the theory is that no explanation is given as to how other types of animals managed to survive. However, as evidence for the event, geologists point to the layers of iridium density at the so-called K-T Boundary – which is the technical term for the boundary between Cretaceous and Tertiary rocks in the Geologic Column. Iridium is an element little observed in the Earth's crust, but plentiful in meteorites.

Now a new theory has suggested that bites from disease-carrying insects may have caused the demise of the dinosaurs. Yet, at first glance, such a theory is no better. Did these particular insects prefer the taste of dinosaurs to other animals? Changes in theories about the demise of dinosaurs are nothing new – when I was at school, my teachers confidently taught us that dinosaurs had died out, because their egg shells had got too thin to survive!

When we accept Genesis as literal truth, the great dinosaur mystery disappears. Most dinosaurs, in common with all other land animals not on the Ark, were killed in the Flood. Many of these were rapidly fossilised by the masses of sedimentation that the Flood would have caused. After the Flood, many of the remaining large reptilian creatures – in common with many other animals – began to die out. That some remained for a long time is illustrated by the many legends that exist about dragons. So a "rapid" disappearance of dinosaurs in rock strata tells us nothing, really, about their extinction. The fact that some scientists are moving away from the scientifically orthodox asteroid impact theory merely underlines that we should have simply accepted the Bible all along.

11

The Floodwaters Abate

In this chapter we are returning to looking at what the Bible actually says about the Flood and how we can understand these events.

The beginning of the end of the Flood is recorded in Genesis 8:1.

God made a wind to pass over the earth, and the waters subsided.

Scientifically, we can divide the effects of the end of the Flood into two. One event would be what happened as the waters gradually abated. After this, there would be another event as the water drained off the newly emerged land. The dynamics of these two events would have been different.

The so-called 'abative' period happened this way:

The fountains of the deep and the windows of heaven were also stopped and the rain from heaven was restrained. And the waters receded continually from the earth. (Genesis 8:2-3)

We have already seen that the 'fountains of the deep' probably refers to massive volcanic activity. If this stopped, then the great movements of the earth's crust would have come to a halt. The 'windows of heaven' refers to sources of water in or above the atmosphere. However, most of the water probably came from the 'fountains of the deep'.

Those of us who believe the Bible are often asked 'so where did all the water go, then?' The answer is simple. It didn't go anywhere. It is still here.

The late underwater explorer, Jacques Cousteau, used to say:

Were the crust of earth to be leveled - with great mountain ranges like the Himalayas and ocean abysses like the Mariana Trench evened out - no land at all would show above the surface of the sea. Earth would be covered by a uniform sheet of water - more than 10,000 feet deep! So overwhelming the ocean seems to be. (Cousteau, J., The Ocean World of Jacques Cousteau - Oasis In Space, Angus & Robertson (U.K.) Ltd. London, England, page17, 1973)

Psalm 104:8 says of the Floodwaters:

They went up over the mountains; They went down into the valleys, To the place which You founded for them.

However, a better translation might be that the mountains were raised and the deeps lowered. Thus, the word translated as 'valleys' might actually be referring to ocean trenches. Cousteau's comment shows that such a movement of land mass and ocean basin could account for where all the water is today.

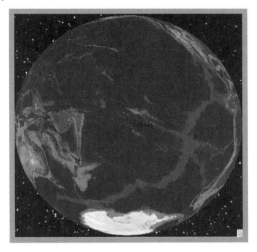

The recession of these waters would lead to the formation of a great deal of sedimentary rock. Much of this could have been laid down on sedimentary rock, which was formed earlier in the Flood, a\nd affected by volcanic and seismic action.

But however interesting the scientific effects of the Flood were, we need to remember why God brought it to an end.

God remembered Noah... (Genesis 8:1)

This is not to imply that God might somehow have forgotten Noah. The verse simply reminds us that God will always keep His promises to us, just as He kept His promise to Noah. He promised to save Noah from the watery destruction of the world, by means of the Ark. He promises to save us from the fiery destruction of the Earth to come, by means of our Ark of Salvation, Jesus Christ.

12

A Raven and a Dove

After about seven months, the Ark came to rest on the mountain. It was another three months, before the waters had receded enough for Noah even to think of taking any action. Imagine the patience that Noah must have had. God had promised Noah that he and his family would be rescued from the Flood, but now the Flood seemed to be over, yet there was still water everywhere.

Perhaps Noah would have liked a supernatural sign, so that he could be absolutely sure what to do next. God often doesn't give us such help—He has given us a brain, and chooses to allow us to use that.

So Noah used two birds in order to determine what was going on outside the Ark. First, he sent a raven. Ravens are scavengers, and the fact that it "kept going to and fro" told Noah that there was some land for the raven—

it couldn't stay in the air forever. However, it did not tell Noah whether the land was fit for habitation yet. That is why he sent out the dove. The dove would need fresh vegetation, and would not be able to scavenge. So the dove came back to the Ark. This indicated to Noah that the land was not yet ready for them to disembark.

Noah waited some more. He then sent the dove again, which returned with a fresh olive sprig. Olives can sprout very quickly, so the appearance of such a plant ought not to be a surprise. However, it told Noah that he could now consider disembarking.

All this information had been gleaned by Noah's own intelligence, and contrasts sharply with the direct instructions that Noah had been given on how to build the Ark before the Flood. Many times, I come across Christians who want a sign, or to "lay out a fleece." Perhaps there is a place for such things, but there is definitely a place for using the thinking-equipment that God gave us, in order to determine answers to problems.

Noah now waited another seven days, before sending the dove out yet again. It is interesting that the word used for waiting is the same word used elsewhere in the Old Testament (e.g. Micah 7:7) to describe waiting in hopeful anticipation for God to work. This is what happened. Soon after the dove had been sent out, and it had become obvious that it was not returning, God told Noah that they could all disembark. During all his time on the Ark, Noah remained faithful. He and his family had been on the Ark, during some dreadful conditions, for 370 days. Noah had been prepared to use his brain, but also to wait for God's timing. This combination of **our** activity and **God's** guidance is an essential blueprint for how we are to conduct our lives as Christians.

13

Giant Mountains and Deeps

Psalm 104:8 says:

They [the flood waters] go up by the mountains; they go down by the valleys unto the place which thou hast founded for them.

Yet the word for valleys can also be translated as deeps, so the passage could be translated:

The mountains rose; the valleys sank down to the place which You established for them. (NASB)

Psalm 104 is referring to the Creation and the Flood. The quoted verse may, therefore, be referring to the land rising and the ocean trenches or deeps lowering as the Flood ended. The last chapter talked about the Flood waters *abating*. Here we can consider what would have happened as the Flood waters *dispersed* from the land, as it rose from the waters. Huge amounts of drainage would have occurred, on a scale never seen since. It is this dispersal of massive amounts of water that could have given rise to many of the world's most spectacular geological features, such as the Grand Canyon in Colorado.

A little closer to home, I recently visited the Giant's Causeway, near Portrush. The information boards at this World Heritage Site declare that the unusual hexagonal columns would have formed over 60 million years ago. How likely is this?

The 60 million year date tag is determined by radiometric dating. Scientists take a sample of rock, and find a radioactive material in it. They measure how much there is of this radioactive material, and also how much of the stable 'daughter' material there is. They assume that they know that the rate of decay of the radioactive material has not changed for millions of years, and that no 'daughter' material was present in the original rock. These assumptions are challengeable. Indeed, many creation scientists have discovered evidence that the radioactive decay rate of uranium, for example, has probably not remained constant.

What happens when you pour molten toffee into cold water? It cracks into strange shapes. This is probably what happened with these mysterious columns. Volcanic material oozed through the crust into the waters of the Flood, and cooled rapidly, cracking as it did. Many of the long columns were probably caused as steam bubbles rose vertically through the molten material. The existence of the hexagonal columns certainly suggests the presence of large quantities of water. Giant's Causeway contains no fewer than seven layers of basalt formation.

Whether the Giant's Causeway, and other geological features, verifies the Bible or evolutionary theory depends on your presuppositions. Christians can have confidence that real, observational science does not contradict God's word. It never will.

14

When the Ice Came

Secular scientists talk a lot about an Ice Age – a period of time when there was massive glaciations over many areas, where ice is not normally found today. Many U-shaped valleys in the islands of Britain and Ireland, for example, show markings somewhat similar to the impressions left today by moving glaciers – 'rivers' of ice.

In the last few chapters, we have examined some of the issues related to the reality of a worldwide global Flood. A study of the so-called Ice Age fits into this discussion.

We have seen that the Flood was not a gentle event, but rather a violent event, accompanied by volcanic eruptions. Such eruptions would have sent dust and aerosol particles into the atmosphere. These could have deflected much of the sun's rays, causing the immediate post-Flood world to become much colder – hence, an Ice Age. Such an event could account for glaciations seen around the world.

Also, the immediate post-Flood world would have had warmer oceans. This would have resulted in greater evaporation of water vapour than today, with correspondingly greater levels of precipitation – much in the form of snow.

Secular scientists suggest an Ice Age lasting about 100,000 years. Meteorologist Michael Oard has shown that such a great length of time is not necessary for glacial geological effects to be produced. His calculations (read about them in the *New Answers Book* from *Answers in Genesis*) show that the Ice Age could be explained by just 200 years of post-Flood history.

Some might argue that the Ice Age is not mentioned in the Bible. Although it is not directly referred to, perhaps it is alluded to by a comment in the book of Job.

> From whose womb comes the ice? And the frost of heaven, who gives it birth? The waters harden like stone, and the surface of the deep is frozen. (Job 38: 29-30)

Job is possibly the oldest book in the Bible to be written, and the events it contains probably happened in the post-Flood world. Was the ice of Job 38 a major worldwide phenomenon, due to the Ice Age?

Much that we might want to say about the Ice Age would be speculation. However, we have once again seen that a belief in the truth of the Bible makes complete sense, in the light of the observed scientific facts.

15

Human Rights for Chimpanzees?

My friends and I used to love to visit the zoo, when we were young. How we used to laugh at the antics of the chimpanzees at their 'tea parties'. We were amused that they wore clothes, as they performed activities that looked vaguely human. Well, we laughed, until sometime later we decided that it was an improper anthropomorphism (i.e., the attribution of human characteristics to animals), and the whole thing was also likely to be distressing to the animals (especially during the training that it took to have them act in certain ways).

The media have recently reported talk of reclassifying chimpanzees, because the researchers claim (wrongly) that chimps are very closely related to humans—even more closely than they are related to great apes, gorillas and orang-utans!

The physical similarities between humans and apes are supposed to be evidence of a common ancestor. These similarities, however, provide equally strong (perhaps stronger) evidence for a common *Designer* rather than a common ancestor. That Designer is, of course, God.

Evolutionists claim that human and chimp DNA are 98.77% similar. Creationist Dr David DeWitt has further shown that even a 1.23% difference in DNA requires 35 million mutations. Such a figure is hardly a ringing endorsement of the idea that chimps and humans are basically the same creature. The use of such statistics is simply done because of the researchers' evolutionary presuppositions, not because this figure actually means anything scientifically. (I recall the famous cliché about lies and statistics.)

Classifying chimpanzees as humans could presumably lead to chimps being granted protection under human rights legislation. For example, imagine how such legislation would have affected the actions of the police dealing with an escaped chimp. In one such incident, a chimp was assumed to be potentially dangerous and was shot dead. Just imagine the headline that might have been: 'Small furry human shot dead!'

Western nations increasingly believe in evolution and reject the book of Genesis. When they believe that man is an evolved animal and closely related to chimps, rather than being God's creation made in the image of God, should we be surprised that researchers come to these kind of conclusions— and that many in society believe the same thing?

16

Our God Contracted to a Span

How will we ever understand the Incarnation? One of my favourite Charles Wesley hymns at least gets close, with these lines:

Our God contracted to a span
Incomprehensibly made Man

The question at issue is this; which Person of the Trinity did the creating? I suggest that it was the Son. In Colossians 1:16, we read:

For by Him (Jesus) all things were created that are in heaven and that are on earth, visible and invisible, whether thrones or dominions or principalities or powers. All things were created through Him and for Him.

Everything was made by Jesus, through Jesus and for Jesus. John's Gospel reminds us:

1 In the beginning was the Word, and the Word was with God, and the Word was God. 2 He was in the beginning with God. 3 All things were made through Him, and without Him nothing was made that was made. 4 In Him was life, and the life was the light of men. 5 And the light shines in the darkness, and the darkness did not comprehend it. (John 1:1-5)

This Word is also the Light. The passage is so famous that we know John is talking about Jesus. Yet Genesis begins with some words of God:

Then God said, "Let there be light"; and there was light. (Genesis 1:3)

The parallel is too striking to be ignored. God the Son was there, right at the creation—indeed, even before it. That is why the Nicene Creed reminds us:

And [we believe] in one Lord Jesus Christ, the only-begotten Son of God, begotten of His Father before all worlds, God of God, Light of Light, very God of very God, begotten, not made, being of one substance with the Father . . .

Yet at the Christmas season, our thoughts are drawn towards a baby.

And she brought forth her firstborn Son, and wrapped Him in swaddling cloths, and laid Him in a manger, because there was no room for them in the inn. (Luke 2:7)

This is the depth of the miracle. In that manger, just a foot or so long, lay the One who had made the universe—the Creator Himself. God contracted to a span indeed!

Wesley says it right, in the same hymn:

See in that Infant's face
The depths of deity,
And labour while ye gaze
To sound the mystery
In vain; ye angels gaze no more,
But fall, and silently adore.

17

Wise Men Came from the East

One of the most enigmatic parts of the traditional Christmas narrative is the arrival of the wise men from the East. Do not misunderstand my use of language. I am not casting doubt that it happened—quite the opposite. It is recorded in the Bible so it happened. However, the biblical account does not suggest that the coming of the wise men happened at the time of the birth of Jesus.

In Luke 2:7, we read that Mary wrapped Jesus in swaddling clothes "and laid Him in a manger, because there was no room in the inn." In Matthew 2:11, however, we read that the wise men found Jesus in a house. It would appear, therefore, that the wise men's arrival took place some time after Jesus' birth. Moreover, Herod, seeking to have this new king destroyed, decreed that all male children two years old and under should be killed

(Matthew 2:16). This is probably not an arbitrary act. After all, Herod, "when he had secretly called the wise men, determined from them what time the star appeared" (v7) and therefore what time Jesus had been born. It would make sense to suggest that Jesus was just under two years old when the wise men came.

Perhaps it had taken the wise men that long eventually to find Jesus. Their reason for having made the journey is clear; "We have seen His star in the East and have come to worship Him" (v2). Traditionally, the wise men are supposed to have followed the star. Yet the scripture doesn't say that. Indeed, it could be suggested that, after initially seeing the star, they didn't see it again, until after meeting with Herod. "Behold, the star which they had seen in the East went before them, till it stood over where the young Child was. When they saw the star, they rejoiced with exceedingly great joy." (vv9,10).

A star that appears and disappears and points the way locally is clearly not a normal star. Suggestions as to the identity of the star have included Halley's Comet, supernovae or conjunctions of planets and stars. Although God could have used any of these, I would respectfully suggest that it is more likely to have been a supernatural event—a star created by God especially for the purpose of announcing the birth of His Son. It is appropriate that God should have used a star, to announce the coming of the Saviour.

The heavens declare the glory of God; And the firmament shows His handiwork. (Psalm 19:1)

18

The Lesser Light

On Day Four of Creation, 'God made two great lights: the greater light to rule the day, and the lesser light to rule the night.' During the month of December 2005, the Moon ruled the night as seldom seen before, rising to a greater height in the sky than had been seen for decades. There were a couple of clear nights where the Moon was out before dusk, yet still clearly visible at dawn.

The Moon has always fascinated me, as it hangs there in the sky. I remember as a child watching on television the exploits of the NASA astronauts landing on the Moon's surface.

The Bible tells us that the Moon is a 'faithful witness' (Psalm 89:37). In what way could it be a faithful witness? Could there be something in some of the old folk tales from around the world. The Australian Aborigines have a story about the Moon dying in a fight with a character of evil. The Moon dies, but rose from the dead on the third day.

Whether this has significance for us is a matter of conjecture. However, the Moon does indeed 'die' once a month—the New Moon period actually lasts three days. This could be compared to the death and resurrection of Jesus. Maybe this is what David is talking about in Psalm 89, when he prophesies:

'Once I have sworn by My holiness; I will not lie to David: His seed shall endure forever like the Moon, Even like the faithful witness in the sky.' (Psalm 89:35-37). The seed of David is referring to Jesus. So the Psalm could be taken as prophetic, perhaps referring to the death and resurrection still to come of Jesus Christ. This would make sense, because Jesus died at Passover. Passover always happens around the time of the New Moon.

I find it endlessly fascinating that the creation itself exists to point us to Jesus Christ. The Apostle Paul says 'Since the creation of the world His invisible attributes are clearly seen, being understood by the things that are made.' (Romans 1:20). Little wonder that he goes on to warn us that we are 'without excuse'. Astrologers and New-Age-types want to worship or revere the Moon itself. But that is not its purpose. Along with everything else, it exists to point us to Christ, through whom alone there is salvation.

19

What were Dinosaurs like?

Most dinosaur fossils are not dug up with all the flesh intact. More often than not, they do not even find all the bones—few fossil skeletons are complete. The bones do not tell us about skin colour, texture etc, or what sex the animal was.

Much of the art of dinosaur reconstruction involves guess-work and disagreement. Often, mistakes are made—for example, the famous *brontosaurus* was actually an *apatosaurus* with the wrong head placed on it!

Some dinosaurs were very big, but most were quite small. The average size of a dinosaur was about the size of a sheep. Frequently, evolutionists scoff at the Bible, saying that dinosaurs could not have fitted in the Ark. However, if we consider that most dinosaurs were small, that all dinosaurs must have been smaller and younger before they grew, and that Noah had only to take two of every *kind*—not two of every *species* aboard, it can be seen that there must have been plenty of room.

Sometimes we are told that dinosaurs do not appear in the Bible. This is not surprising, as the King James Version was published in 1611, but the word dinosaur was not invented until 1841. However, maybe passages referring to dragons in the Bible, and in other ancient literature and legends, refer to dinosaurs. The *behemoth* in Job 40 is unlikely to have been either an elephant or a hippopotamus, as suggested in some footnotes, because neither of these beasts has "a tail like a cedar". Rather, the description seems to be closer to that of a sauropod, such as apatosaurus.

We do not need to try to fit dinosaurs into the Bible. Instead, we use the Bible to interpret our observations about dinosaurs. For example, dinosaurs were land animals; land animals were created on day six; so dinosaurs were created on day six. Therefore, we should not worry about dinosaurs. At *Answers in Genesis*, we often refer to them as "missionary lizards", because we can use these examples of God's creation to help present the Gospel.

20

Five Years On

The events of September 11th 2001 (9/11) are etched on my mind. I know precisely what I was doing on that day, when the aeroplanes were crashed into the Twin Towers. I was planning my father's funeral.

Frank Taylor had passed away on Sunday September 9th 2001, after a long and painful struggle with mesophelioma—lung cancer caused by industrial asbestos. A quiet man, his ministry to me was in his encouragement. Just four days before his death, I had been showing him the digital camera I had bought, for the web design business that I was then involved in. In my childhood, I remember helping him in the darkroom in the cellar, as we developed black and white photos together from his camera. As I showed him how images could be manipulated through software, his eyes lit up, as we once again shared the joy of developing photographs.

Less than a year after I became a Christian in my teens, I came across creationism. I read a book, whose message was that Genesis was true. As a teenager, studying science A-levels[1], this was mind-blowing stuff. Could the Bible actually be so real that it connected with issues that I was studying?

I gave the book to Dad for him to read. He was equally bowled over by it. His reaction was this: "I find it completely convincing". The one person in the world, whose opinion I respected more than any other, was equally convinced by the truth of God's word, as I was. At that stage, we knew no other creationists personally, but we knew that God's word actually mattered to real-life issues like science. If Dad had been the slightest bit sceptical, I might not have got into the ministry, to which God has now called me.

---

1 A-levels are school leaving exams taken in most parts of the UK (England, Wales and Northern Ireland), usually at the age of 18

As one of God's quieter, but faithful servants, my father was, as we all are, victims of the most dreadful event to befall humanity. The events of 9/11 were truly dreadful, and the suffering caused was immense—yet everyone who died in that terrorist outrage would have died one day in any case. But there was a more awful event, near the beginning of history, when one man, who happened to be the ancestor and representative of all of us, disobeyed God and broke the one commandment that God had given him. Before that event, there was no death in the world. Why did Dad have to suffer so much? It was because Adam brought sin and death into the world. Dad was a victim of that event, as we all are, and as we all are active participants in the rebellion that brought the sentence of death. Likewise, so were those who lost their lives in the events of 9/11. But some of those victims knew what Dad knew—that their faith in Jesus Christ has saved them. Although we live in a world of sin, suffering and death, we know that that Jesus' death and resurrection has destroyed the power of sin and death in our lives, if we will turn to Him in repentance and faith.

21

Is It a Planet?

Newspapers have recently been concerned over the status of the object in the Solar System known as Pluto. Is it a planet? Or is it some lesser type of object?

Pluto has been problematic since its discovery in 1930 by Clyde Tombaugh. Astronomers were actually looking for a large gas giant planet, similar to Uranus and Neptune, which they believed was causing perturbations in the orbits of the other two planets. When Pluto was discovered, it was quickly realised that this was not the gas giant being sought. Today, we know that Pluto is very tiny—smaller even than the Moon. It is really a double planet, as Pluto and its moon Charon together orbit a common centre of gravity.

Recently, a new object, given the unromantic temporary name of UB313, has been discovered, which is larger than Pluto. A number of other so-called Trans-Neptunian Objects (TNOs) have been found, which are only very slightly smaller than Pluto.

Reports on August 16th 2006 suggested that the International Astronomical Union (IAU) might make a new classification for planet which would define Pluto as a planet, and also UB313, Charon and Ceres, the largest asteroid. In the event, the IAU surprised everyone by removing Pluto's planetary status altogether, meaning that future science textbooks will once again list only eight planets—Mercury, Venus, Earth, Mars, Jupiter, Saturn, Uranus and Neptune.

Early national newspaper reports speculated on what the increase or decrease in planetary numbers might do to the practice of astrology, and interviewed astrologers for their opinions. Astrology is, at best, nothing more than a pseudo-science, though many Christians, this columnist included, view it as a dangerous form of occultism. But why did the newspapers not interview Christians for their views? Have Christians got nothing to say about the universe?

In the Bible, the Universe has a number of purposes. It was made by God on Day Four of the Creation Week in order to teach us the extent of God's blessings (Genesis 22:16), to glorify God (Psalm 19:1) and to be of help to us (Genesis 1:14). God created Pluto. UB313[1] has not yet been given a name by the IAU, but God knows what its name is (Psalm 147:4). What a great God we have!

---

1 Since writing this article, the IAU has officially named this object as Eris.

22

Animals After the Flood

If the Ark landed somewhere in the Middle East, then all the animals would have disembarked at that point, including animals that we do not find in the Middle East today, or in the fossil record in that area. How did kangaroos get to Australia, or kiwis to New Zealand? How did polar bears get to North America and penguins to Antarctica?

The biblical principles that we can establish are that, after the Flood, the ecological reconstruction of the world, including its vulnerable animal kinds, was what God wanted to happen, and the animals must have spread out from a mountainous region known as Ararat.

One accusation thrown at biblical creationists is that kangaroos could not have "hopped" to Australia, because there are no fossils of kangaroos on the way. However, fossilization is rare. One ought likewise to ask why it is that, despite the fact that millions of bison used to roam the prairies of North America, hardly any bison fossils are found there. Similarly, lion fossils are not found in Israel, even though we know that lions once lived there!

Comparisons can be made with more modern recolonisations. For example, the Encyclopædia Britannica has the following to say about Surtsey Island and Krakatoa.

> Six months after the eruption of a volcano on the island of Surtsey off the coast of Iceland in 1963, the island had been colonized by a few bacteria, moulds, insects, and birds. Within about a year of the eruption of a volcano on the island of Krakatoa in the tropical Pacific in 1883, a few grass species, insects, and vertebrates had taken hold.[1]

Some animals could have floated on vegetation rafts. Some could have been taken by people and introduced. Savolainen *et. al.* have suggested, for example, that all Australian dingoes are descended from a single female domesticated dog from South East Asia.[2] A third explanation of possible migration is that animals could have crossed land bridges. Such land bridges may have occurred, if there was an Ice Age after the Flood, as suggested by retired meteorologist and Ice Age researcher, Michael Oard.[3]

Such severe climatic changes could have been the catalyst that would encourage certain species to develop or migrate in certain directions. These severe changes could also account for some of the many extinctions that

---

1 **community ecology**. (2006). In *Encyclopædia Britannica*. Retrieved July 20, 2006, from Encyclopædia Britannica Premium Service: http://www.britannica.com/eb/article-70601

2 Savolainen, P. et al. *A detailed picture of the origin of the Australian dingo, obtained from the study of mitochondrial DNA,* PNAS (Proceedings of the National Academy of Sciences of the United States of America), Aug 2004; 101: 12387 - 12390

3 Oard has published many articles in journals, and on the AiG and ICR websites, on these issues. For a detailed account of his findings, see his book: Oard, M. (2002), *An Ice Age Caused by the Genesis Flood,* (California: Institute for Creation Research)

there have been. Additionally, his studies provide a model for how land bridges could have developed.

Some still remain sceptical about the idea of land bridges all the way to Australia. Nevertheless, by a combination of methods that we see today, including land bridges, there are rational explanations as to how animals may have got to far flung corners such as Australia. Of course, we were not there at the time to witness how this migration may have happened. Those adhering to a biblical worldview can be certain of these facts:

Animals obviously did get to far flung places like Australia.
There are rational ways in which it could have happened.

We should therefore have no problem in accepting the Bible as true. Creationist scientific models of animal migration are equally as valid as evolutionary models, if not more so. The reason such models are rejected is because they do not fit in with the orthodox, secular evolutionary worldview.

[*There is an extended explanation of how animals could have recolonised the earth after the Flood, in the* New Answers Book, *available from* Answers in Genesis]

23

Northern Lights

Speaking in Shetland earlier this year, I asked my hosts if they ever saw the Northern Lights (technical term *Aurora Borealis*). At the time, we were driving back from an evening meeting. They answered that they often had views of the Northern Lights, and that there had been a particularly good display about three years previous. As we reached the end of the road, where their house was situated, in a remote part of the island, it was apparent that there was a glow coming from the North. We extinguished all lights and walked to the end of the track, and stood in awe for a couple of hours at one of the most fascinating and beautiful sights in nature.

The Sun is emitting a so-called *solar wind*, comprising of free electrons and positively-charged ions. The solar wind streams in all directions at a velocity of about 400 km/s. The Earth has a magnetic field – which explains why compasses point North. The North-seeking pole, or Magnetic North Pole, is situated not at the normal North pole, but currently near Ellesmere Island in Canada. The Earth is basically like a big magnet, and north poles of magnets point towards this Magnetic North Pole. Since North Poles of magnets are always attracted towards other magnets' South Poles, it follows that the Earth's Magnetic North Pole is really a South Pole!

Readers who remember learning about how electric motors work in school physics lessons will appreciate that electrically charged particles, like those in the solar wind, will be affected by magnetic fields. Thus, solar wind particles are channelled towards the Magnetic North Pole. The energy produced by this funnelling causes excitation of atoms in the air, which therefore give off light, in a very similar manner to the light discharge of a fluorescent light tube, or a neon light. As most of the atoms affected are oxygen, the Aurora often shows colours characteristic of electrical effects on oxygen – a blue-green, and a red colour. The effect is stunningly beautiful, especially as the effect is frequently accompanied by movement of the lights-glows. In the display, which I saw, the light was very light green, and moved in what looked like folds of a curtain.

Why does the Earth have a magnetic field? One of its functions appears to be to deflect harmful solar radiation. Also, the north-seeking effect of magnets can be used for navigational purposes. It is notable that God created astronomical effects "for signs and seasons, and for days and years" (Genesis 1:14). Both the magnetic effect, and the position of stars, has been used in past times for navigation. Also, the deflection of harmful radiation makes the earth more habitable, in line with Isaiah 45:18, where God declares that He is the One "Who formed it to be inhabited".

Why are the Northern Lights so beautiful? The answer to this would appear to reside with God's purpose in creativity. When we see the beauty of

God's creation, through the Northern Lights, through the beauty of planets, stars, galaxies and nebulae, we are reminded of Revelation 4:11.

You are worthy, O Lord, To receive glory and honour and power; For You created all things, And by Your will they exist and were created.

24

Creation in Science Lessons

Good science teachers encourage their pupils to think for themselves. It was arch-atheist Richard Dawkins (Simonyi Professor for the Public Understanding of Science) who said "Science is a discipline of investigation and constructive doubt."[1] Few would disagree with this analysis; though many of us would disagree with his next sentence:"Faith demands a positive suspension of the critical faculties." Romans 12:2 does not urge us to be transformed by the *removal* of our minds.

Three parts of the United Kingdom use the National Curriculum (NC). Science NC documents all recommend the teaching of scientific controversies. In Wales, in the section headed "The Nature of Science", it states that "Pupils should be taught… to recognise that scientific controversies arise from different interpretations and emphases placed on information."[2] The

---

1 Dawkins, R., *The Root of all Evil?*, TV programme, January 9th 2006, Channel 4
2 Science: The National Curriculum in Wales, ACCAC, 2000, p38

Northern Ireland NC states: "They should study examples of scientific controversies and the ways in which scientific ideas developed. Pupils should be encouraged to distinguish between claims and arguments which are based on scientific considerations and those which are not, and to recognise the provisional nature of scientific explanations."[3] Meanwhile, the Science NC document for England urges that pupils be taught "ways in which scientific work may be affected by the contexts in which it takes place [for example social, historical, moral and spiritual]."[4]

If pupils are being taught about a topic such as nuclear power, it defies logic to suppose that they would not be taught that there are differing viewpoints on the subject. Similarly, environmental issues would be accompanied by healthy classroom discussion.

When a teacher approaches the subject of origins, it is disingenuous for them to give pupils the impression that the question is closed, and that evolution is proved. Even the most radically atheist teacher should acknowledge that there are eminent scientists who do not accept neo-Darwinism. The NC statements quoted suggest that discussion of the subject of origins should take place, as an example of scientific controversy and of the contexts in which scientific research takes place.

This is an issue, about which Christian parents should care. The Bible places the responsibility for education at the feet of parents, not the state. We need to hold our children's schools accountable for the way our children are taught, and what they are taught. God will hold us accountable for the education our children receive.

---

3 Northern Ireland Science National Curriculum, p26
4 Science: The National Curriculum for England, QCA, 1999, p46

25

Dawkins Deconstructed

With the publication of Richard Dawkins's new book, *The God Delusion*, we now have an expanded version of his atheist manifesto. One would have at least hoped that he would have taken the opportunity to present a more intellectually rigorous case. For my part, I was looking forward to getting to grips with an intellectual argument. I was to be disappointed.

Dawkins' arguments, far from having intellectual clout, are mostly like this example: "The argument will be so familiar, I needn't document it further."

Dawkin's paucity of argument is best illustrated by his poor use of logic.

Poor Logic

Examine this extraordinary sentence.

Although Jesus probably existed, reputable biblical scholars do not in general regard the New Testament (and obviously not the Old Testament) as a reliable record of what actually happened in history, and I shall not consider the Bible further as evidence for any kind of deity. (p97)

Look first at the use of the word "probably" in "Although Jesus probably existed". Why is Dawkins doubting this fact? There is no question that Jesus existed. It is illogical to add the word "probably".

Look next at the use of the word "reputable". What is a "reputable biblical scholar"? The test of reputation has been left undone by Dawkins. Presumably, a "reputable biblical scholar" is one who agrees with Dawkins' attempts to rubbish the Bible. Such people can be found, though whether the adjective "reputable" is appropriate for such people is a matter of opinion. In our opinion, a "reputable biblical scholar" is one who approaches the Bible with respect, believing it to be the inspired, inerrant and authoritative word of God, from the very first verse.

Thirdly, why is it "obvious" that the Old Testament should not be regarded as reliable? He has clearly not read a detailed apologetics of scriptural inerrancy, such as that provided by Brian Edwards in his masterly book, *Nothing But The Truth*.[1] That is again down to his presupposition, that evolution is true so Genesis is wrong so evolution is true. Merely making a statement, or using the word "obvious", does not make a statement true, when it is not true. Just from these three points, we see that there is no logical reason given by Dawkins for rejecting the use of the Bible as evidence.

An important element in the use of logic is to recognise *logical fallacies*. One such fallacy, frequently used by Dawkins, is the *Ad Hominem Attack*.

---

1 Edwards, B., *Nothing But The Truth*, (Third Edition), (Evangelical Press: 2006)

Ad Hominem

This sort of fallacy involves attacking the opponent instead of the argument—"playing the man instead of the ball".

There are several examples of this. There is a particularly nasty attack on a schoolteacher, who happens to be a creationist. Notice, on page 95, how Dawkins describes certain American educational establishments.

> He moved up the hierarchy of American universities, from rock bottom at the "Moody Bible Institute", through Wheaton College (a little bit higher on the scale, but still the alma mater of Billy Graham) to Princeton in the world-beating class at the top. (p95)

Why are the three institutions arranged hierarchically? What is the basis for Dawkins assessment of standards at each place? He doesn't say, but we assume that it is to do with belief in the Bible. Why is it implied that, because they number Billy Graham among their alumni, that this is a negative for Wheaton College?

The book is full of such examples.

Conclusion

Christians have nothing to fear from this book. Far from being a reasoned argument for atheism, it is a hysterical rant. It would be appropriate for Christians to be aware of the principal arguments of the book, and how they are countered. Maybe there will one day emerge a book that has a little more intellectual rigour. Even an intellectually rigorous apologetic for atheism would not concern us; God is a God of wisdom and reason. Dawkins' new book is weak, even by atheist standards.

26

Quite Interesting Human Evolution Tale

Viewers of Stephen Fry's TV Quiz, QI (which stands for "Quite Interesting"), might also have read the companion book, "The Book of General Ignorance" by John Lloyd and John Mitchinson. It is an entertaining, if only semi-factual read, containing as it does some outrageous examples of evolutionary fairy stories.

The section on "What did human beings evolve from?" is worthy of mention. Lose 10,000 points if you answered "apes" or "monkeys", if you are an evolutionist – though quite what evolutionists think the distinction is between a common ancestor with the apes and an actual ape we never seem to get told! According to this book, "He lived in the Pliocene era, eight to five million years ago. This creature descended from squirrel-like tree-shrews, which in turn evolved from hedgehogs, and before that, starfish."

The book goes on to suggest that "one of the first populations outside Africa were the Andaman islanders." Lloyd and Mitchinson go on to describe the simplicity of the islanders, clearly implying that they are less evolved than we are. This is very much in line with the less polite opinions of Charles Darwin himself.

> On the last page of his book *The Descent of Man*, Darwin expressed the opinion that he would rather be descended from a monkey than from a 'savage.' He used the words savage, low, and degraded to describe the American Indians, the Andaman Island Pygmies, and the representatives of almost every ethnic group whose physical appearance and culture differed from his own . . . . [In this way] Charles Darwin labelled 'the low and degraded inhabitants of the Andaman Islands' in his book *The Descent of Man*.[1]

Lloyd and Mitchinson go on to express surprise at their "familiar idea of God."

> Their supreme deity, Puluga, is invisible, eternal, immortal, all-knowing, the creator of everything except evil; he is angered by sin and offers comfort to those in distress. To punish men for their wrongdoing he sent a great flood.

We should not be so surprised. Far from being lower in evolutionary terms, these Andamanian people have probably simply been isolated for a long time since colonising the island after the Flood. After all, the Bible makes clear that we are all descended from one man, Adam, and therefore all of one race—the Human Race. They have retained much of their knowledge of the truth of who God is. And that fact really is Quite Interesting.

---

1 Jean-Pierre Hallet, *Pygmy Kitabu*, Random House, New York, pp. 292, 358–359, 1973

27

The Holy Spirit in Creation

In the Lancashire cotton mill town where I grew up, Whitsunday—occurring this year on May 27th—was an occasion for celebration. It involved a walk of witness around the town by many churches. Other non-biblical traditions grew up, such as the Whitsun brass band competitions. For many children, the day was second in excitement only to Christmas, because on Whitsunday, children would receive presents of new clothes, and then the Sunday afternoon would involve the traditional Sunday School outing, with picnics and games. As a small child in the 1920s, my mother vividly remembers her worst Whitsun, when she ruined her brand new clothes, by falling into a pond during the Sunday School outing!

Traditionally, Whitsunday—or Pentecost, to give it its biblical name— is that point on the church calendar when the coming of the Holy Spirit in

Acts 2 is celebrated—at least in those churches that observe the church calendar. It is followed a week later by Trinity Sunday. What may be a surprise to people is to find that the doctrines of the Holy Spirit and the Trinity do not begin in the New Testament, but, once understood, can clearly be seen in the words of Genesis 1.

We know that God created the world using a six day process, rather than instantaneously. That is why, when we read that God made the earth "without form and void", it is incompleteness which is implied, not corruption. It seems that God created the material ex nihili first, without any energy. It is at that point that we read "the Spirit of God was hovering over the face of the waters." The Holy Spirit seems to be energising the formless, void materials. Thus the Spirit is intimately involved with the creation process.

The various elements of creation came into being when we read "God said...". It is Jesus who is described as the Word of God, and in Colossians 1:16, we read about Jesus: "For by Him all things were created that are in heaven and that are on earth, visible and invisible, whether thrones or dominions or principalities or powers. All things were created through Him and for Him."

That the Son and the Spirit, as well as God the Father, were intimately involved in creation, yet that there is only one God, is a reinforcement of the doctrine of the Trinity. The season of Whitsun and Trinity Sunday might be an appropriate time for us to remember that the whole Bible tells us of the nature of God.

28

Pride Comes Before the Fall

They say that pride comes before a fall—though this is actually a slight misquotation of Proverbs 16:18: "Pride goeth before destruction, and an haughty spirit before a fall." Pride was certainly the issue that led to the Fall of Satan, or, as Isaiah 14:12 calls him, Lucifer.

> How art thou fallen from heaven, O Lucifer, son of the morning! how art thou cut down to the ground, which didst weaken the nations! For thou hast said in thine heart, I will ascend into heaven, I will exalt my throne above the stars of God: I will sit also upon the mount of the congregation, in the sides of the north: I will ascend above the heights of the clouds; I will be like the most High. (Isaiah 14:12-14)

Part of his sin appears to be his belief that he could be "like the Most High". There is a pride and arrogance in these words, which is indicative of his state of mind.

Yet Satan, in common with the rest of creation, must have been created good. According to Genesis 1, when God looked at everything that He had made, it was "very good". This must include Satan. Indeed, his creation as a perfect angel is hinted at in Ezekiel 28:15. "Thou wast perfect in thy ways from the day that thou wast created, till iniquity was found in thee". Satan was not from eternity past. Jesus says that Satan was "from the beginning" (John 8:44), but Satan did not precede that beginning – unlike Jesus himself (Ephesians 1:4).

Satan's sin of pride also includes the belief that he could "ascend" to God's current position. This suggests two beliefs on Satan's part. First, that he has the ability to increase his own standing to become like God. Second, that God himself must have followed the same route to gain His current position. Satan's beliefs about himself and about God indicate a form of upward evolutionary thinking. In a sense, this is the very beginning of the theory of evolution – a belief that life processes have developed in an upward manner, without direct intervention by God.

Such a view is contradicted by the facts of Genesis. Genesis (and therefore the whole bible) starts with the words "In the beginning, God..." God does not have a beginning. He does not have a cause. God is Himself the cause of everything. The Bible wastes no time attempting to prove the existence of God, because His existence is taken as self-evident. ("He that cometh to God must believe that he is." Hebrews 11:6) God has not evolved into His current position—He has always been the Most High. In the same way, we cannot develop to become gods in our own right. That was part of the lie that Satan used in his temptation of Eve (Genesis 3:5).

The whole concept of evolution is not to be seen merely as a mild aberration, or misconception of the truth. Nor is it to be seen as a mechanism which God could have used as He created the universe. Rather it is to be seen as an attempt to deny God the glory for who He is and what He has done. This is one of the many reasons why Christians need to be clear on what they believe about the book of Genesis.